Love and Transcendence
Second Edition

ROSEMARY C. HYDE

Copyright © 2017, 2021 by Rosemary C. Hyde
Cover Design © 2021 by Evelyn Rainey

All rights reserved. No part of this book may be reproduced, scanned, or distributed in any printed, audio or electronic form without permission. Such piracy of copyrighted materials is a violation of the author's rights and is punishable by law.

ISBN-13: 978-1-946469-04-5

Sheltering Tree . Earth Publishing
PO Box 973
Eagle Lake, FL 33839

ShelteringTree.Earth/writer-guidelines

DEDICATION

Ellen on her 75th birthday

CONTENTS

Foreword	i
Looking November 14	1
Tumbled Rock November 14	2
Today's Email November 15	3
The Sun Still Shining November 15	4
Worthwhile November 16	5
I See You Walking November 16	6
The Plunge November 16	7
Molecules November 17	8
Seeds of Love November 17	9
Relearning November 17	10
We Were We November 18	11
Cat Lessons November 19	13
Breathe November 19	14
Prank? November 19	15
Freedom November 20	17
Winter November 21	18
Bozo the Clown November 21	19
Habits November 21	20
Prisms November 22	22

Who I Am November 23	23
Twining November 24	24
Wonderland November 24	25
Fear November 24	26
Walking November 25	27
Swirling November 26	28
Risk of Loving November 27	29
A Time for Everything November 28	30
I'll Clean Up! November 28	31
Co-Creating November 29	32
Respiration November 30	33
Meditation December 1	34
Pea Soup December 1	35
Cauldron December 2	36
Dictation December 2	37
The Real Ellen December 3	38
Moving Ahead? December 4	40
Party Eve December 5	41
Your Party December 6	42
Spirit Gift December 7	43
Beauty Beheld December 8	44
A Life's Worth December 8	45

Night December 9	46
Closet Memories December 10	47
Letdown December 10	49
Widow December 10	50
Attachment December 10	51
Integration December 11	52
Love December 12	53
Dream Trip December 12	54
Giving and Receiving December 13	55
Grief December 13	56
Waves of Grief December 13	57
Elusive Sleep December 14	58
New York Winter December 15	59
Reframing December 15	62
Progressive December 16	63
Junk Mail December 17	64
Money December 17	65
Filling Ellen's Shoes December 18	66
"Ellen Loved" December 19	68
Light Bearer December 20	69
Hanukkah and Solstice December 21	70
Every Step With You December 22	71

Blind Navigation December 23	73
Christmas Spirit Present December 24	74
Christmas Night December 25	76
Christmas Joy December 25	77
Grazing December 26	78
Meanings of Odd December 27	79
Electronic Images December 27	80
Opposites Attract December 28	81
Hospital Dream December 29	82
Happy December 30	83
New Year's Eve December 31	84
Afterword	85
Afterword July 2021	88
About the Author	96
Discussion Guide	99

FOREWORD

These poems chronicle a major transition. They portray the roller coaster experience of seven weeks of grieving. Their order has no rhyme or logic. The poems remain in the order in which they were written, at random moments of inspiration, during the last two months of 2008, ending exactly eight years ago today.

Ellen Scheiner, M.D., was a soulmate for me. She was 67 in 1998 when we met online. I was 59. I was Irish Catholic, and had grown up in Rhode Island. Ellen had been born and had grown up in Brooklyn, child of Jewish refugees from Russian pogroms. She had spent a significant part of her childhood not at home but as a patient in the St. Giles Hospital for Crippled Children in Brooklyn, where she learned to admire the surgeons who sought to repair, even a little, the devastating paralysis and deformity of her right arm, which had been torn from its shoulder socket during her breech birth. From the devoted Episcopalian nuns who ran the hospital, she learned to appreciate Christian ceremonies, holidays, and music. In the doctors, she found role models. When discussing the harrowing obstacles to achieving her life goals as a physician, she often, half-jokingly, commented on her potential as an amazing token of every acknowledged disadvantage save color – visibly disabled, female, homosexual, Jewish. Though marginalized on these fronts, she created and defined herself, and found a way to live the life she dreamed of, as successful physician, generous philanthropist, and caring friend.

When Ellen and I met, we had both experienced first relationships that had endured for decades without digging deep into our souls. Neither of us had experienced, with our parents or in our adult lives, healthy, balanced love that transcended ego to embrace eternity. We agreed, upon committing to be each other's life partner, to have a psychologist coaching each one of us. The dueling psychologists were very helpful. Weekly, we'd both go to our respective sessions, and then return home to share what each therapeutic conversation had revealed.

Although our love for each other was deep, neither one of us had managed to transcend our resentments from childhood. Consequently, we both, repeatedly, fell into the twin traps of transference and projection. We didn't understand why, suddenly, in the middle of a loving conversation, either one of us – or, more often, both – could find herself hurtling into Hell – beset by hurt feelings, inchoate anger, painful despair. With the help of the psychologists in our respective corners, we finally, slowly, learned that in these moments, we were re-experiencing the despair of our early childhoods. Once that became clear, there was no way we wanted to go back there any longer, and we were able to ignore the triggers and stay in the present with our adult selves.

Then my psychologist insisted that I get the book <u>Ethnicity and Family Therapy</u>, which detailed the unconscious behaviors that people brought into adulthood from childhoods experienced in different cultural cauldrons. Through that book, Ellen and I learned that 90% of the misunderstandings we were still experiencing stemmed from not recognizing each other's culturally based attitudes and behaviors.

This whole process took approximately three years, and then we were able to move ahead as one. We built a practice together, Ellen as psychotherapist and I as classical homeopath, working with the same clients. Into the nine years we were together, we packed a lifetime of rich relationship. For the first time, both of us understood the power of marriage. For the first time, we learned to love unconditionally. For the first time, we reaped the gifts of giving 100% to each other – not just 50/50.

We tried repeatedly, through the early 2000s, to be recognized as spouses. Once, we were joyfully married in Portland, OR, only to become one of over 8000 couples whose marriages were summarily and involuntarily dissolved by the Oregon Supreme Court almost a year later. Finally, in 2008, Massachusetts amended its same sex marriage rules to allow couples to marry there who did not reside in Massachusetts. On September 11, 2008, finally, Ellen and I were able to marry, on a tiny beach in Padanaram Village, where I had lived as a child. We were deeply happy finally joined together as one.

On the eve of our first commitment ceremony in Berkeley, CA in 2000, Ellen received a blood test report stating that her breast cancer, which had been treated years before, had returned, and was now metastatic. She had a prognosis of about six months to live. We looked at each other, and decided that yes, we would go through with our commitment to each other, and live every moment and every day as fully as we possibly could. We were fortunate to have another eight years together. She died in 2008, suddenly, from cardiac arrest, slightly less than two months after our pilgrimage to be married in Massachusetts.

During the time we were together, including two or three crises during which her life seemed about to end, we had built exceptional closeness through a deep and rich range of experiences starting in New York, continuing for six years in Berkeley, CA, and finally, moving to Chapel Hill, NC, where my daughter had settled and married, to be close to our two grandsons, Avery and Julian. It was good, after our time on the "Left Coast" – where the ocean, though wonderful, was on the wrong side of the land – to return to the East Coast whose rhythms and culture we remembered from childhood. Moving back east to North Carolina, to be near my daughter's family, was also a loving gift to me from Ellen, who, because of her cancer, knew that I would most likely outlive her (although we always acknowledged that one can't know these things ahead of time). Unfortunately, suburbia, and the softer affect of people from the southeast, were hard on Ellen, the acerbic, quintessential Manhattanite.

Ellen died, suddenly, the night of November 4 to November 5, 2008, after waiting long enough to assure that Obama had been elected president. She hadn't felt very well that day and had gone to bed early. We thought she had a virus. She felt queasy and unsteady on her feet, and I had helped her get her slippers on when she had needed to use the bathroom. We were watching the election returns on television, and she was dozing as the vote counting extended into the early morning hours. Every once in a while, she'd wake up and ask me how the returns were coming in nationally. We'd have a conversation about what was happening with the election, and she'd go back to sleep. At around 2:30 am, I had just seen that Obama's election was official. She woke up and asked again, and I was able to give her the good news. We were elated, cheered, hugged each other, and had a conversation about how wonderful it was that Obama had won, and how promising it felt to be finished with Bush's endless wars and the financial downturn that was then evolving.

Then Ellen said she needed to use the bathroom again, and I went around to her side of the bed, and knelt to put on her slippers. I put the first one on easily, and then the second one just wouldn't go on. I said, "I can't seem to get this slipper on!" and looked up at her. I realized instantly that, sitting on the side of the bed, she was gone, between one slipper and the next! I laid her body down in the bed, and called 911. Over the phone, the dispatcher coached me through five minutes of intensive rapid compressions until the EMTs arrived. There was no sign of response to the compressions, and the EMT crew told me she was definitely gone, which I knew. Her heart had just stopped, between beats.

The police, who had arrived with the EMTs, shoved a phone

book open to the funeral services page in front of me, and instructed me to choose a mortuary to come and take the body. I was able to rouse her oncologist who gave me instructions on how to transport the body to the UNC Cancer Center, so that the cancerous tissues could be harvested to serve as research materials, as had previously been agreed. So the hearse deposited her body at UNC, and then, a week later, after an autopsy had been performed and the tissues harvested, the same mortuary picked up the body for cremation. I had had virtually no time before the body was taken from the house (feet first, as she had specified!) to compose my thoughts and say good-bye. At my request, the morticians kindly allowed me to spend some time with the body at the mortuary before cremation. I was grateful. The autopsy showed no plausible cause of death, other than spontaneous cardiac arrest. The cancer was present, but not in a way that would impede vital functioning anywhere. And although sometimes Ellen did not feel well, she was still vitally engaged in living every day all day.

I think it was just time. Ellen was an ardent practitioner of Vipassana Buddhism, and she practiced regularly with her teacher. As an outcome of her spiritual work, Ellen had finally been able to forgive everyone, including her mother, and she was practically glowing. Everyone who saw her commented on how wonderful she looked. Of course – she was preparing to leave. She was probably not conscious of what was happening. She was just feeling happy and complete.

Ellen had often said she didn't believe in an afterlife. She believed that when someone died, that was the end. But apparently she was very surprised. Within 6 hours of her death, she was able to activate her own phone line and voicemail to communicate to me (wordlessly) that she was in Paradise. And I became aware, over the following weeks and months, of her spirit's loving and supportive presence growing in my awareness. I learned that love doesn't end with the passage from physical embodiment, and that learning this truth is an important step on the path toward integrating a transformed self that is capable of moving on into new life and new awareness.

The dream that ends my seven-week grief story, as told in these poems, was prophetic. The dramatic shock and suffering I experienced, along with my disorientation after Ellen died became an entrance into a completely different, more beautiful life for me. Accepting what was, giving up my attachment to the life Ellen and I had shared, and opening my heart to new possibilities gave me new love, new opportunities, and a new career that I love – in my seventies.

When Ellen died, I looked frantically on line and in bookstores for someone else's experience to learn from during those first weeks of grieving. I found scholarly explanations of the patterns of grief, and religious homilies on how to survive it, but no writing that emanated from the heartfelt moments of shock I was feeling immediately after losing my beloved. I thought I was going crazy because the experience was so bizarre, so uneven, and so jarring. From one minute to the next I careened from peace to despair to feeling lost to anger to sentimentality – all of it extreme and unpredictable. My body was first numb, then screaming in pain. I felt, heard, and saw strange lights, voices, and impressions that I knew were real but that seemed insane. My whole being was torn open.

After the first few days of frantically searching for a guide through this wilderness, I started writing, conscious that only during the experience itself would it be possible create an account of how it feels to open to grieving. I recognized that I had the opportunity only in that moment to create the testimonial I had been seeking. As a Certified Classical Homeopath in practice for over ten years, I was well aware of the homeopathic principle that "Like Cures Like."

Based on this principle, I knew that the vicarious experience of my grief would be soothing to other readers going through their own grieving, not only for lost loved ones, but lost abilities, lost opportunities, lost dreams. Grief is a universal human experience. Opening wide to it, rather than resisting, brings one through to the peace that awaits on the other side. Grief and sorrow, well lived, are gifts in disguise. I wrote these poems with the intention of creating and sharing a healing experience with others who might be searching for solace, as I had been.

My experience, through those first weeks, became this collection of poems. As a bereavement counselor, I have shared the collection with others in acute grief (I now am a Board Certified Chaplain, among other new skills and roles). Those with whom I have shared these poems have found the experience of reading them – usually in one sitting – therapeutic, calming, and helpful. I offer them to you now, in that spirit, both as balm if you are tossing on the waves of immediate grieving, and as a stimulus to insight and self-awareness if you seek to know vicariously what is, undoubtedly, one of life's ultimate and most amazing adventures. As you consciously journey into grief, may you gain healing and insight into your own unresolved losses, so that you begin to experience the light that awaits you as you return to gratitude and forgiveness.

Rev. Rosemary C. Hyde, Ph.D., CCH, BCCC
Board Certified in Classical Homeopathy and Clinical Chaplaincy
Co-Minister, Unity Center of Peace, Chapel Hill, NC.
December 31, 2016

LOOKING NOVEMBER 14

Labor Day 1999, East Village apartment building,
Elevator door opens to dark landing
Revealing my Love, my Bubbele – our first meeting,
Tall, gray hair, beatific smile, surrounded by bright light –
Her loving aura.
Hazel eyes the same color as mine,
Our hearts beat faster, instantly smitten.
Inside, we sit facing, till wee morning hours,
Only looking into each other's eyes,
Wordlessly, insatiably absorbing each other,
Imbibing the wonder, the heart, the depths,
Becoming one overnight.
Nine years later – after brief but total unity, lives entwined –
Every moment, every day spent together –
I look at her cool dead shell, her strong, peaceful face, her energy gone.
My heart beats faster, overflows with loss and love. Tears stream.
Love is eternal.

TUMBLED ROCKS NOVEMBER 14

Our hearts and souls deeply united –
Sharing insights, observations, love of words,
Discovering the path to wisdom hand in hand, soul to soul.
Nine years of transformation,
Tumbled rocks polishing each other, revealing hidden value,
brilliant hues, greater love,
Smoothing away rough spots and dull coatings,
Sparking into trifling spats, to find embedded gems,
Transforming each other forever, revealing the divine.

TODAY'S E-MAIL NOVEMBER 15

My beloved,
Today, I got your e-mail
From two months ago –
You sent "An infinite supply of hugs"
Saved up against the now
When you have gone,
When I so need embrace,
Your warm breath, your beating heart.
How did you send me that today, knowing?

THE SUN STILL SHINING NOVEMBER 15

Dark, windy midday.
The swirling leaves and dust
Echo sadness in my soul.
Clouds part, and instantly I bathe in stunning light.
The sun was always there, shining, though I couldn't know.
I mourn losing my Love,
The house echoing emptiness.
But she is still there, somewhere, beaming.
I robe myself in her rays.

WORTHWHILE NOVEMBER 16

I think of when we first moved here –
Our first mail, first greetings to neighbors,
Excitement over a new house, new friends.
Today, your ashes sit silent,
The house achingly empty.
Your books, dishes, glasses, robe
Sit, discarded, no one's – as now am I.

I SEE YOU WALKING NOVEMBER 16

I'm surrounded by my family's love,
By friends' concerns,
Trying to carry on,
But weeping, sobbing unexpected tears.
I see you freed now – striding, gamboling,
And frisking with beloved pets.
You are released of pain and hindrance, you are light and whole,
Strolling arm in arm with friends and loved ones,
Looking back to assure that all goes well with me.
At least I feel content to carry in my heart that
Comforting and hopeful image of my Love.

THE PLUNGE NOVEMBER 16

Shock. Unreality. Daze.
Nothing is the same.
I don't recognize myself.
The world is upside down, blurred and wavy.
I've plunged into a deep, dark sea,
Spiraling downward,
Carried by momentum,
Not breathing, not daring to,
Sensing myself from a distance
   In shadowy green.

MOLECULES NOVEMBER 17

You said your remaining molecules would care about me.
That was comforting.
You said we are always exchanging molecules –
That they leap constantly from one person to the next.
When you died, your molecules suffused me.
But, still alive, they keep leaping, from me to others.
Always shifting, changing.
They must move along.
Already, in two weeks, so many changes.
I miss you! You left, and I didn't.
You are in my mind and heart, but Memory quickly stiffens,
like an old scar.

SEEDS OF LOVE NOVEMBER 17

Your word, your look, could penetrate the soul,
Your questions piercing to the heart of sadness, giving others hope.
You always knew each person's deepest self.
For many who were touched by you, Angel of light,
Those seeds of love echoed forward
In lives better and truer.

RELEARNING NOVEMBER 17

You always lit the fires, loved the dancing flames, the rays of warmth.
Tonight, first snow of the season.
To honor you, I light a fire on the hearth.
Smoke billows out, alarms clamor, telephone rings,
Should I call the fire department?
No, No! No fire, just smoke. Closed flue. Fanning,
Open windows and doors. It's OK.
Alarm won't turn off –   too much smoke.
I cough, chase the dog outside.
Finally, I get the flue to open.
Are you laughing at me, tenderly?

WE WERE WE NOVEMBER 18

Today, autopsy done, I got to see your shell.

I wanted to look at your face a little longer, to be able to let you go as
it felt right.

I had to leave, though – it was time.

I know your face no longer is you, that you have emerged a fully endowed, beautiful,
graceful, spirit from the bent and battered body that shaped your earthly life.

I indulge the image of us as kindred disembodied spirits, flitting around each other outside earthly weight,

Eternally bonded in the dimensionless ether, in pure spirit.

Here, embodied, our souls sang forth unearthly harmonies in every mode.

Melodies of our pure love and pure creation,
Each of us unique and also complementary to the other,

Bracketing our songs with dissonance, and clashing over minor daily chores.

Such an irony!

We made both harmony and clanging conflict.
In the process, we created sparks of love in many hearts,

Building communities, inspiring people to love greatly.

    There certainly was a "We."

CAT LESSONS NOVEMBER 19

Haiku grieves. He hides. He fasts. He mopes.
He misses his person.
He doesn't know what to do with himself –
Disoriented, confused, forsaken.
I grieve. I hide. I fast. I mope.
I, too, miss my person, my Bubbele.
Time passes, and I know not when I am.
What hour? What day? When was I supposed to leave?
Why can't I find my stuff and get out the door?
Did you tell me something? Where did I just put that down?
Haiku meets a new friend, and seems miraculously cured –
playful, hungry,
comfortable.
I will need a lot more than a new friend,
But watching Haiku relax, I know I will need to move on in turn,
    Accepting what is, and living again.

BREATHE! NOVEMBER 19

Today, a bodywork session
Asking me to relax into gravity,
Breathing deeply, accepting.
Especially accepting.
After forty minutes I feel better
Than I have in two weeks.
Grief strangles muscles, spirit,
Brings grasping pain
Magically relieved with help,
    Impossible to fathom alone.

PRANK? NOVEMBER 19

OK – Let's see how this works.

We need other people.

We need love.

It's more important than anything: more than food, water, shelter,
sanitation, heat.

When we develop friendship and relationship, we feel happy and
fulfilled.

Our life curls comfortably around our connection with the other, which is
really a connection with our Self in the Divine.

We share suffering, joy, laughter, waking and sleeping, relaxing.

Then life gets yanked away – the other dies.

I sit in shock, wondering how to move. My life is broken.

Is something there beyond this life on earth?

If love is not forever, why do we feel it at all?

Why then does it make our life splendid and worthwhile?

Is this a cruel prank? Or am I not seeing what's real?

FREEDOM NOVEMBER 20

I study your favorite picture –
Your left arm raised high, standing in the waves,
Happy Ocean dweller, my Dolphin.
I see you now, free, healed, two handed –
Both hands waving, frolicking in the surf,
Happy. Back straight. Pain lifted.
Whole-breasted warrior woman. Runner.
Angel. Joy in motion.

WINTER NOVEMBER 21

Transformation, rest,
The appearance of death.
Not dead, but fallow, lying silent.
We two were one.
With you gone, my leaves shrivel, drop.
My heart a winter wood,
Waiting for new life.

BOZO THE CLOWN NOVEMBER 21

Punch! Bam! Biff!

Rock. Spin. Bounce.

Bruise. Cry. Hurt.

Always smile.

Stick it out.

Grief.

HABITS NOVEMBER 21

Habits comfort us.

We enjoy our routines – getting up, stretching,

Brushing teeth, showering,

Smelling that first warm brew of morning.

Our movements are precise –

Two steps here and three there. Get a glass and dish on the way by.

Turn left, reach into the drawer for a spoon,

Not needing to look – Practiced motions effortlessly repeated,

Choreographed,

A fluent sequence

Of graceful, entwined, well learned movements.

Now, suddenly, I'm alone.

The dance has vanished.

Like a disconnected marionette, I turn aimlessly.

Right, then left, forward then back,

Wondering, confused: "What now?"

"Where's that spoon?"

"What comes next?"

PRISMS NOVEMBER 22

You survive now as a prism,
Pieces scattered, in me, in friends, in family,
In places we've shared.
Shards of memory.
Kaleidoscope of tumbling moments.
Chiseled glass parsing rays of love in rainbow tints.
I recognize you in a phrase, a moment, a chance event
But long to hold you whole, to feel your warmth, your breath,
Your kiss.

WHO I AM NOVEMBER 23

We.
I.
Immense gulf between the two!
Rosemary and Ellen – Roellen – one identity, one energy. We.
Now I must learn to say "I," foreswearing "we."
But "our" life continues, our selves stay merged,
Our souls forever bathed in the becoming of shared love;
Even if one can no longer see "us" – only "me."

TWINING NOVEMBER 24

Grapevines,
Twining,
Shaped for years around each other,
Supporting, mirroring, touching, caressing.
Inseparable –
My self remains enlaced with yours.

ROSEMARY C. HYDE

WONDERLAND NOVEMBER 24

Down the rabbit hole.
In a heartbeat total change – it's weird.
The white rabbit: late, late!
The tea party, babbled nonsense,
The Cheshire cat grinning – at what?
The red queen playing croquet – Off with her head!

When you left, I went down the rabbit hole – unfamiliar
chaos in my soul, my mind, my life.
I can't remember if Alice escaped.
Mind-altered nightmare.
Will it end?

FEAR NOVEMBER 24

I am alone, as many people are.
At night, fear closes in.
I feel small, fragile,
Like a nestling dislodged, hungry, flightless.
What will happen to me – alone and old and sick?
If I die, will we be as one again? Will you come for me, care for me?
Will I feel again the wondrous peace of loving union?

WALKING NOVEMBER 25

Walking in morning air – brisk, sunny, beautiful –
I connect with the world,
Love the light,
Resonate to winter stillness.
I recognize, too, life from other spheres,
Connecting with all that lies outside this present moment.
Remembering that nothing is lost that has been,
And that I am wrapped in endless love.

SWIRLING NOVEMBER 26

Tossing, crashing waves.
Crackling, devouring flames.
Wind-driven clouds, pregnant with power.
Nature's restless energy, snapping and surging –
Gusts, tides, gales, inferno.
Same rhythms, same swirls as in my heart and mind.

RISK OF LOVING NOVEMBER 27

We were committed – married.
To have and to hold, in sickness and in health,
Till death.
To share our hearts and minds, our thoughts and feelings,
Till compassion.
To live, laugh, and love together
Till joy.
To think and study together
Till wisdom.
To walk together on life's path,
Hand in hand, soul in soul, apart but united.
By turns blissful, sad.
Within our joy of union lay the pain of separation,
The shift from day to night, from bliss to ache,
The rhythm of our passage across time –
    The price of loving.

A TIME FOR EVERYTHING NOVEMBER 28

Your heart stopped.
You stepped out of the pulsing rhythm of life.
I helped you put on one slipper, and then you left – Gone!
No more shifting seasons, ticking clocks, waking and sleeping.
Steady breathing – stopped.
No more rising and falling, lying and standing, rest and action.
It happened so suddenly, so easily.
Was it because your whole life skirted the rhythms –
Asymmetrical, outsider, were you already on the edge?

I'LL CLEAN UP! NOVEMBER 28

"I'll clean up!"
You always said that with such goodhearted cheer!
I could not believe how you enjoyed cleaning,
Making things beautiful again,
Respecting their substance
And their makers.
Tonight, I'm frying hamburger alone, grease flying.
Then my tears mix with soap, making salty suds
As I wipe the skillet and the stove,
Missing your cheerful "I'll clean up!"

CO-CREATING NOVEMBER 29

Two minds, two hearts, three hands...
One spirit, creating one life for our time together.
Two houses, two kitchens, two histories, two professions
Unified in us, in our space, our aura.
We were Not one, Not two –
Instead something other, beautiful, hopeful, more –
We lived the love that humans long for in their deepest hearts.
Now you are there, and I am here – Still united.
We sit astride, one foot on earth, the other where?
I wonder how to be in two places.

RESPIRATION NOVEMBER 30

I wake each morning, the sound of dog and cat breath in my ears,
My heart leaping up to greet you before I see you are not there beside me.
I give thanks for these furry creatures who share my breath,
Living souls who knew and loved you, too.
I rise and spend my days learning to find you everywhere in spirit.
To know that all I meet exchange your love with me,
That love is what I now must learn to breathe.

MEDITATION DECEMBER 1

I'm learning.
After meditating as duty, requirement, task,
Toil to attain calm,
Now I see how meditating links me
With what is,
With spirit, love – limitless, beyond matter.
And with you.
What I call "real" is just a dream,
My made-up view cocoons within my single self;
Peering from the spyholes of my eyes,
But I'm not seeing from the vastness of my soul.

PEA SOUP DECEMBER 1

I talk and talk. I try to listen,
To hear what I need to hear,
To learn what comes next, what to expect.
But no one tells me.
Maybe I talk too much. Maybe I look as though I know
What I'm doing, as though I'm "coping beautifully."
What does that mean?
It's like a thick fog,
A white-out.
I look about, and see only my own foot and hand.
As once in the Alps, after a Sky-Tram ride,
Snow everywhere, all white.
If I move, will I fall off an unseen edge?
Will I lose the inn?
I have no idea where to turn;
No safety, no path, no knowing –
– Nothing. All blank.

CAULDRON DECEMBER 2

Bubbling, boiling, thick brown stew
In iron cauldron –
My thoughts.
I peer in.
A potato bubbles up:
I must remember it.
But then it sinks back out of sight,
Followed by a pea, a carrot, an onion –
All there one moment, gone the next –
My thoughts.

DICTATION DECEMBER 2

One hand useless, you couldn't type,
You, so full of words and thoughts.
So you dictated and I typed for you.
Last night, you had me type again.
Your words and thoughts were clear and crisp.
So loving, so supportive,
Following a well-learned channel
From that plane to this.
Deep consolation
From cosmic e-mail!

THE REAL ELLEN DECEMBER 3

Who is the real person?
I look at your pictures, read your poems,
Listen to what people say about you.
I think of you, a young doctor, thrilled
To help people, to be important, to count in the world.
I reflect on your mission to create compassion for the dying.
I wonder at your sensitivity to suffering and to beauty, to language and music,
At your adeptness – not disabled,
At your ready wit and play with words,
At your transcendent poetry,
At your impromptu, silly, amazing morning songs,
At the crushing pain you carried with you always, though never giving in,
At the wealth of life and joy you gave each moment.
I think of our time together –
Our peace, our fights,
The minutes and the years when just
Being together filled all the crannies

Of our hearts with love
As if we'd drunk pure soul food.
I am smitten with you more and more.
How could one person be so much, so many?

MOVING AHEAD? DECEMBER 4

In two days, we'll hold the cocktail party memorial you requested.
Putting it together has been good –
A project, something to distract me,
To share with others.
But then what?
Then will it be time to move on,
To claim my life, to find new friends, to live alone?
But I'm not ready.
I feel on a planet by myself,
With no echo to my calls.
I feel muffled in cotton, unable to move, a mummy,
All gladness gone, all purpose fled.
I feel left.

PARTY EVE DECEMBER 5

Convivial.
Friends and family from next door and out of town.
Plans, excitement,
Rented glasses and plates stacked high.
The eve of Ellen's oft-requested
Memorial cocktail party.
She saw packed rooms, gourmet food,
Perfect Rob Roys and martinis,
A "classic" party, as she was proud of giving
In her beloved New York loft –
Moved now to this more gentle place she came to live,
The South. Suburbia.
Tears will flow amid the cocktails,
As we delight in having shared her love.

YOUR PARTY DECEMBER 6

It's over. The house was full,
The bar active, the food abundant, a Feast.
New friendships budded and old ones swelled.
I know you joined us as we celebrated knowing you,
Rejoiced that you'd been born,
Wept at losing you.
I wore your scarf, your earrings, your bracelet,
The jacket you gave me.
They made me feel closer to you,
Armored with your strength,
Embraced within your love.
We made the party you had pictured,
Knowing that its love would draw us all together
In a warm circle, friends.

SPIRIT GIFT DECEMBER 7

What happens when many people meet
To hail the life and love of one
Whose path has led beyond this earth?
Jesus told his friends to gather in his name and he would be with them.
When they did, they were transformed.
I always thought that only happened if you were God.
Yet, yesterday, your loved ones came together,
Shared one room, one breath, one feast, one toast –
Blessing. Honoring. Remembering. Learning.
You too were here,
Present in our hearts and minds.
Your spirit lifted ours above our daily fears.
We communed – a sacred moment,
A hint of bliss to come
When we too leave this life,
A moment of unity with what is.
We will always remember that we shared
Your special moment, your party,
Your gift of love.

BEAUTY BEHELD DECEMBER 8

Your grandson, age 5, says in recalling you,
"I like the way she looked."
He loved you.
We find beauty where we love.
I undress and shower, look at my body
That has always felt ugly
But that you thought beautiful.
You loved me,
Seeing beauty is the surest sign of love.
I miss your love!
I remember, when we first met, searching your face
And feeling pity that you had to bear that nose, large and hooked,
Not knowing or seeing that the body parts you didn't love
Were your scarred chest, bent back, and small, useless arm.
Yet I found your beauty arresting.
Seeing you made my heart race.
I loved you!

A LIFE'S WORTH DECEMBER 8

You always thought no one liked you,
No one appreciated your struggle, disabled in an able world,
No one understood how hard you worked to keep up.
You felt set aside, marginal.
You felt shame and failure.
But when you died, people said you had inspired them,
Helped them, showed them they could succeed as you had done,
Against such odds.
Why don't we learn, when young, to tell our admiration
To bravely be ourselves, saying what we really feel?

NIGHT DECEMBER 9

Too much!
Sadness.
Tasks.
Changes.
Worries.
Weariness.
Missing you!
Tears.
Must stop and go to bed!

CLOSET MEMORIES DECEMBER 10

Time to look through closets and
Sort clothes, bags, shoes, jewelry,
Making room for life continuing.
Each item recalls a different story –
A life history on coat hangers.
The ultra suede skirts perfectly
Hand made with graceful pleats –
Proud elegance under white coat and stethoscope.
The men's bathrobe, stylish, from Saks
Found on a sale table for a song –
Your dress for a posh party – prankish delight.
The burnished cowhide satchel – professional power bag –
Carry-on for conference presentations –
Commanding authority.
The sale dress you bought
To wear in scorching Midwest summer heat
For my daughter's wedding – cool, unwrinkled, matriarchal.
The Lucy Cavendish Cambridge College scarf,
Blue stripes on black –

Pride of friendship with a don.
Every piece a different memory, added story,
How can I discard these markers of your life?
For the next owner, they'll be just fabric, leather –
Virgin stuff, stripped of memory and meaning.

LETDOWN DECEMBER 10

Suddenly, I'm tired, alone.
Your memorial now is past,
Friends have thought of you and moved on,
Telling me to come along.
But I can't move with them.
My life is too altered, too strange, too alone,
Our special closeness vaporized.
I attend a seminar on grief, and
Have to leave.
I think of losing you and sob.
I'm asked where I am I on the "healing scale of 1 to 10."
– Elsewhere.

WIDOW DECEMBER 10

Widow. Widow's weeds. The merry widow.
Black widow spider. Widow-maker. Widow's Walk.
Widow –
What a strange-sounding word!
I've known it all my life.
I've never understood
Its aloneness, sorrow, slow moving stupor,
Its feeling of being sliced in half, axed.
No longer joined in daily life and love,
Condemned to wander, always missing, always wistful for what was.

ATTACHMENT DECEMBER 10

Grief is a way of staying close to you, of
Not moving on.
With you I was happy – moving on is sad.
How can I stay united with you
If I stop thinking of you?
How can I think of you without missing you?
How can I miss you and not grieve?
For over 60 years I yearned to find you, and you me.
Then ten short, beautiful years – our lifetime together.
I am grateful. And bereft.

INTEGRATION DECEMBER 11

How do I integrate?
I want to stay connected with you,
And I need to find me.
I look for one path forward,
But I have double vision – two roads, forking.
Where are the 3-D glasses, red and green,
That I can wear to see again both life and love
United, deep, and whole?

LOVE DECEMBER 12

I knew how much you loved me
Finding your old account list today –
Scribbled pages, nameless passwords,
Penciled crudely at all angles –
Indecipherable. Impossible to use.
You'd used it for years.
But next to your computer, you had laid for me to find
A new, typed, ordered list with
Usernames, passwords, id codes
Meticulously noted, logically laid out, stapled together.
You typed this when typing was painful,
When you felt tired and weak.
You thought of me and showed your love –
A splendid gift.

DREAM TRIP DECEMBER 12

Last night, I knew I'd been there before.
Every night for a while, now,
I'm traveling, traveling –
In trains, all night, wearily pushing on;
Finding myself in strange, lonely stations
Riding alone in empty cars
All over the world,
Always searching,
Looking for my lost mate.
Where has she gone?
I seek her energy, her love, her familiar smell,
Her loving gaze.
Surely I'll find her somewhere!

GIVING AND RECEIVING DECEMBER 13

Energy moves. It creates itself
When I give attention and love to others,
It comes back to me.
Like a cosmic game of catch, sending the ball back and forth, over and over.
I was taught to return the ball always, never to keep it,
Never to enjoy it for myself.
Daring never to believe I could be loved.
But you saw into me and still wanted me.
I am comforted, beloved.

GRIEF DECEMBER 13

Though, inevitably, we mourn the loss of every love,
We fear grief.
We try to hide the thought.
We stay too busy, captured by daily tasks –
Laundry, cleaning, shopping, mowing, trimming, arranging, working –
We call this "life."
Yet we ache for deeper realms,
Where love and grief alike await.
As the hidden side of love,
Grief too must bring its gift –
Its transcendent view of life conjoined with death,
Its hint of liberation and reunion with what is,
Inner passageway to Joy.

WAVES OF GRIEF DECEMBER 13

People have told me grief comes in waves.
I feel its surf pounding on the structure of my life,
Here, eroding – destroying strength and calm;
There, depositing – covering up who I was before.
Steady rhythm of breath, of life –
Moving the very sand of self,
Creating new birth, memorable "firsts,"
Sculpting the me who will live on, alone.

ELUSIVE SLEEP DECEMBER 14

I'm tired, weary.
It's been five weeks since you left.
But sleep stays just out of reach,
Eluding my exhaustion,
Like a shimmering oasis
Dancing afar before my eyes,
Sweet rest that I will never find.

NEW YORK WINTER DECEMBER 15

We traveled back and forth, thinking we could be bicoastal,
And I'm so glad I had that chance to live with you
In your beloved loft, your neighborhood, your building,
Learning a little what it meant to be, like you, a New Yorker.

I think of:
That first Christmas, shlepping the six-foot spruce
From the corner grocery, down the street, and up the elevator,
Boots, mittens, knitted scarves and hats shielding us from knifing wind.
Then decorating, in our first shared spell of Christmas magic.

The stiff courtesy of doormen, stationed all day, all night, – hailing, guarding, helping.
Your stories of asking the doormen to put on your earrings or button your shirts
Because, one-handed, you couldn't.

The icy drafts stabbing in through lofty windows, impossible to block,
Making us set the heat to 80 so we didn't freeze.

The friendly firefighters in the station down the street, smiling and waving
As we walked by to the barber, the cleaner, the grocery, the deli.

The purity and quiet of fresh city snow, so quickly blackened.

The surprise of glancing from the 7th floor
To see yellow cabs everywhere, sole traffic, horns honking.

The sound of sirens through the night, background symphony to sleep.

The excitement of walking to a busy restaurant or hailing a cab to Lincoln Center,
Of passing stalls selling items you later said you "got on the street."
Walking, wondering, past cracked brick houses and regal brownstones in The Village,
Exploring the Green Market with its winter New York produce –
City moments, always hustled, elbowing with others.

The naked fear of cancer checkups at Sloan Kettering,
Where everyone – respectful – called you "Dr. Scheiner."

The intimacy of spending all day and night together,
burrowed in your loft –
15 foot ceilings and classic modern furniture, like a photo in
House Beautiful.

The pleasure of sitting side by side in black leather chairs,
Cheerful morning sun warming our heads and arms
As together we read the New York Times and drank fragrant
coffee.

The tender moments spent cuddled,
Immersed in each other, before the crackling fireplace,
Bach Inventions gently pouring over us.

The bare emptiness of that beloved loft
When, off to California,
We sat side by side on kitchen chairs, all else taken by the
movers,
Floors and walls starkly clean,
Seeing our honeymoon suite for one last time
Before flying, excited, to our new house:
To the life we would build together.

Now you've gone alone to your next venture,
And I wrap around me that first season's precious memories,
To help warm me through this long and solitary winter.

REFRAMING DECEMBER 15

I'm on a stormy ride with no map, no seatbelt,
No way of knowing what comes next.
As on a wild coaster, carried up and down,
Whipped around sharp angles,
Spinning off, flying out.
Will I limp away as victim – haunted, injured?
Or will I rather grasp adventure,
Be transformed?

PROGRESSIVE DECEMBER 16

As people live, they evolve.
Their awareness changes –
Each new experience bringing new insights.
They say soulmates remain connected, eternally.
Do you keep learning with me
On my always lively daily path?
Do I get to learn with you in your new home?
How does that work?
Do we evolve together, even when apart,
Like paired electrons across continents?
I hope so!

JUNK MAIL DECEMBER 17

I never thought I'd welcome junk mail!
But your name is still there.
Life seems normal again when I sort the day's envelopes.
The wacky errors we used to laugh about –
The middle initial you acquired on a list and never lost,
The mixups of my name and yours.
It's sad to discard these worthless papers sent to you –
Undeliverable.

MONEY DECEMBER 17

When we were two – two incomes, two accounts –
We felt safe, taken care of. Enough margin.
Now, after your death, financial free fall.
The banks are stressed and no one has time to say
What will happen to our money.
Your monthly income gone.
Our plans in disarray.
Is this our social penance for loving each other, two women?

FILLING ELLEN'S SHOES DECEMBER 18

When we first met, and you took me to visit your neighbor,
We were sitting, chatting, on her couch,
And suddenly she asked me "Are you wearing Ellen's clothes?"
Such a strange question! We laughed.
You and I had just met, and I was dressed as me.
But we were the same size, we shopped at the same sites,
And we often liked the same things.
When catalogues came, we raced to see who looked and ordered first,
Who got what we both liked.
Now, I AM wearing your clothes.
I feel closer to you; I feel protected; I honor your memory.
A week after you died, new shoes you'd ordered for yourself arrived.
I tried them on. They fit. They looked great.
I kept them, didn't send them back.
They seemed to have some meaning, coming when they did.
I'm still learning how to fill your shoes in other ways,

LOVE AND TRANSCENDENCE

How to be as loving, friendly, lively, engaged in life
As you modeled for me.
How to meditate and connect with the divine
As you showed me.
How to inspire love in others
As you did in me.

"ELLEN LOVED" DECEMBER 19

As people send their loving thoughts of you
For your Memory Book,
I learn your genius in their shared words:
"Ellen loved."
You told me that you thought
People were disappointed in you
Because disabled, worn out from trying harder,
You produced less work.
In fact, people instantly
Saw your love for them, your caring,
Your generous urge to help them grow and learn.
You didn't disappoint – you inspired.
You were a true friend.
Did I learn well enough from you
To carry forth your love, your legacy?

LIGHT BEARER DECEMBER 20

Your last name, Scheiner, meant "light bearer,"
And your first name, Ellen, meant "light."
You were called a "lightning rod,"
A conduit for people's feelings.
I think of you those last two months –
You glowed with life. You were transcendent.
You radiated, as death approached.
You achieved peace, you were serene,
You had forgiven.
You were glass
Focusing the light of love,
Searing it into us.

HANAKKAH AND SOLSTICE DECEMBER 21

Tonight, I lit a Menorah candle to honor you,
To show my love – a tiny point of light
Shining in the wintry gloom.
First day of Hanukkah, celebrating light.
It's also winter Solstice,
The day of least light, least warmth.
I sense the unending –
That you are truly gone,
Not coming back.
That life is darker, harder.
I never saw how deep and final losing you would be,
How I would miss my Sun.

EVERY STEP WITH YOU DECEMBER 22

Every morning, we made the bed together,
A ballet duet, matched step by step.
Together grasping sheet, then blanket,
Arranging them just so.
Now only one side is disarranged,
And I jerk the covers carelessly.

So many little movements built
Our daily waltz together,
Synchronized with ease –
Answering the door and telephone,
Grooming the dog,
Cooking dinner and cleaning up,
Planning evenings, outings, parties.
Sitting together in our leather chairs
Reading Sunday papers;
Choosing when to relax indoors or out,
The ritual of sitting down at 5, drink in hand, to talk –
Partners in the daily dance of life.

Now I do these things alone,
Shared harmony missing,
My ears hissing loudly in the silence.

BLIND NAVIGATION DECEMBER 23

Suddenly alone –
It's like navigating in a fog:
Shoals loom and stormy tears flood in –
Shipwreck hazards, Unseen, unmapped.

As if now blinded,
I seek new and other senses,
Guides to harbor peace.

CHRISTMAS SPIRIT PRESENT DECEMBER 24

I dreamed a Christmas service.
My favorite childhood priest was there.
He always helped me, made me feel special, as did you.
He told me
To run up and ring the steeple bell.
Other bells were pealing forth and
Our voice, too, was needed.
I ran up, as told, gripped the rope, and pulled.
Nothing.
I climbed higher. Twigs and grass fell from the bell.
It wouldn't ring. Then I got really close, and saw
Inside the bell a nest of budgies –
Eager, bright green birds, about to fledge,
To spread the Word to many.
I helped them fly away. I was happy.
I did my job, felt its meaning.
I had feared an agonizing Christmas
As I mourned your absence.
Instead, as in the Christmas story,

LOVE AND TRANSCENDENCE

I feel warmed by others.
The bell rings out.
The Word is love, and I am blessed.

ROSEMARY C. HYDE

CHRISTMAS NIGHT DECEMBER 25

I sit in my chair, alone, Christmas music in the air.
No light in your chair's corner.
Holiday tunes add to the silence.
When I went to play a disk of carols today,
I found in the machine the B-Minor Mass –
Last melody you heard,
Acutely tuned to your heart's wish.
Are you hearing now music more divine than Bach's,
Or can we listen here together?

CHRISTMAS JOY DECEMBER 25

Little boys, intense excitement,
Craving the new.
Christmas anticipation.
Watching them, I understand
My remembered childhood hurry for Christmas.
It came too slowly – too eagerly awaited.
Now I yearn to reunite with you –
My future Christmas.

GRAZING DECEMBER 26

Today was your favorite kind of day –
You called it "grazing."
No appointments, no have-tos, no pressure.
A "day off" doing only what comes to mind.
Finally, today I had no calendar, and
I "grazed," thinking of your glee
When you had this chance.
I see now your insight in tasting bliss,
Aware that one day of grazing makes but a
Spot of order
In the weedy infestation of tasks.
Delight requires staying in the Now,
Focusing on each move like a Zen Master,
Loving the beauty of simple work well done.

MEANINGS OF ODD DECEMBER 27

A friend said, "This must have been an odd holiday."
What an unusual word to use!
But so true – everything was strange, including how I see myself.
I was not alone, thanks to family, but I missed my Love.
The day seemed weird, abnormal – anomalous.
Odd is all those things and
Also means not paired – alone –
Peculiarly, I have now become odd:
Mateless, like an odd sock,
Victim of vicissitude.

ELECTRONIC IMAGES DECEMBER 27

Photographs, videos, recordings –
Together, we made these objects
Carelessly, thoughtlessly – for fun.
Now, suddenly, they are treasures of you,
More precious than gold or jewels.
I seek them, hoard them, play them, view them,
Wondering how I didn't
Know each moment's painful joy or
Feel stabbing pleasure in each second we were close,
As now I feel the razor slash of losing you.

OPPOSITES ATTRACT DECEMBER 28

I sit in meditation,
Breathing deeply, softly, evenly,
Watching swaying trees, knowing I depend on them.
I inhale vital oxygen, produced by plants.
I exhale then what they breathe in.
Opposites.

Like plants and vertebrates,
You and I sustained each other.
You, physician, scientist, activist, New Yorker, Jewish;
I, teacher, homeopath, ethnographer, small town Irish Catholic.

Our love became as air, life-giving.
Opposites, we breathed together.

ROSEMARY C. HYDE

HOSPITAL DREAM DECEMBER 29

I felt you in my dream last night.
You were in a hospital,
Alone in a room, where you had died.
But you weren't dead.
Your molecules radiated love and energy,
Enfolding me, though I could not be with you.
I felt joy.
You let me know that when I meditate,
When I think of you, you feel my love
And I bring joy to you as well.
When I awoke, I thanked you for that loving moment.
It was heavenly!

HAPPY DECEMBER 30

Today I felt happy. It was strange.
I haven't enjoyed reading a book or article,
Listening to beautiful music,
Basking in warm sunshine,
Or seeing good friends
For weeks now, since you left.
Where did the happy feeling come from?
Why did it come?
I think the dream in which you beamed me love
Helped me find a center, a place of peace,
Showed me that while we're in different places
We're still connected,
That love goes on, and always will.
I felt happy when I awoke,
    Richer in love, replenished, blessed.

NEW YEAR'S EVE DECEMBER 31

I'm watching "Live from Lincoln Center":
Interview with Loren Maazel.
Maestro Maazel observes, about retiring,
"Life is all about Beginnings and Endings."

This New Year's Eve marks the end –
The last hours
Of the last year we shared.
And it signals the beginning –
The first moments
Of what I will be next time when I grow up –
My graduation from your school of love,
   My soul's moment to unfurl and soar.

AFTERWORD

Feelings are our soul's weather. It is all too easy to assume that what we are feeling will go on indefinitely, but indeed, even during the first few weeks of my plunge into screaming sorrow, my emotions, like clouds, scudded and morphed from moment to moment. I careened from immobilization to raw, inflamed pain. One moment I was lost and the next, open to learning. Sometimes I was physically grounded while at other times, I felt disconnected from earthly experience. But profound loss colored every moment. It was hard to imagine I could ever again experience serenity or joy.

The big lesson of that moment was to understand that life's events carry with them potential gifts in proportion to their impact. As the Tao teaches, every experience reveals polarities. As the Buddha taught, our attachments lie at the source of suffering. As Jesus taught, love is eternal and we cannot lose it. I learned that the closer I have become to someone, the more my self-awareness is intertwined with that person, as hers is in me. Therefore, when Ellen and I found ourselves no longer on the same plane of existence, a big part of my heart remained with her. In return, I also gained and was challenged to integrate into a new self what remained with me of her gifts. To go forward, I had to experience rebirth. I had to learn and accept the new polarities that I took away from our severed earthly relationship, while also detaching from my previous experience of unity, one on one, with my soulmate. I needed to learn that the part of my self-identity from which I felt sundered lives on in a different, non-physical realm. I had to perceive and become the full new, integrated person that I now could be.

I had in the past experienced griefs that had required similar transformations – they just hadn't been quite as catastrophic as this one. Always, eventually, I had found a new equilibrium in transformed awareness. Like a tree fractured by lightning, I had not died, but had adapted and become stronger. This time, too, integration and transcendence awaited.

From among the shards of my fragmented self after Ellen's transition, a new awareness started to emerge. I discovered that my sensitivity to spiritual energy was now much closer to the surface than ever before. I found that, at will, I could now go within to contact and enjoy the inner peace of meditation. I also knew, now, how to express that spiritual connection in words – much more clearly than I ever could before. I found in myself a clarified mirror of compassion capable of perceiving in others the love of Spirit that I share with everyone on earth. I discerned a much stronger ability to understand the wordless knowing that often manifests in my consciousness to guide my choices and inform my decisions. I finally heard and answered the call to spiritual leadership that had echoed through my whole life from my first stint in the Catholic convent starting at age 16, and I took action to enroll in seminary and complete my ordination as an Interspiritual minister.

In learning, finally, to say "YES" – freely – to the presence of Spirit in my mind and heart, I have discovered myself living a whole new life, one I never imagined could be possible. In this life, I am bathed in the light of divine love and the peace of oneness with the I AM that is Spirit.

My life, today, is filled with joy and gratitude. I am grateful I was led to understand the nature of my grief after Ellen's unexpected death, and then inspired to surrender to what is. In a way, losing her became for me a near-death experience. Classically, the experience of dying and coming back to earthly life leads one to abandon fear and to embrace Love. I was blessed indeed. I wish a similar level of blessing to all of you who read these poems, process your own griefs, and surrender all fear of what is real about life.

Durham, North Carolina
December 31, 2016

Afterword July 21, 2021

Yes, there is new life after a tragic loss. Over time, I realized that Ellen's and my shared love was still present, even between dimensions of awareness.

During the first six months or so after Ellen had departed this physical dimension, I was very aware that she still felt deeply connected to me. For instance, by the end of the first full day of our separation, I discovered that Ellen's phone line had accumulated seven messages, all from the same number: 777-777-7777. When I listened to the messages, I heard only deep, primal silence. What??!! I Googled the number and learned that it didn't have a listing anywhere in the world. But there it was – seven times in a single day on Ellen's phone, attached to blank messages. Her phone had not rung, or surely I would have heard it at least once. I had been there all day. Weird!!!

The number did not exist in the physical dimension. I had to begin thinking that perhaps Ellen – who had been brilliant in adapting and using technology and was way ahead of the curve in creating ways to use cell phone technology – might be the source of these messages. Finally, I began to wonder what the number 7 meant! I researched and discovered the mystical meaning of 7 in Judaic tradition: it refers to the highest circle of Heaven. Ellen, like many Jewish people, had vigorously disavowed while alive any belief in an afterlife. These seven messages on her line from that non-existent phone number composed only of sevens might mean that she had been surprised after leaving her body, perceiving she was still aware– and she wanted to let me know!

Over the next several months, occasional messages also came through on her discontinued email account, which she seemed still able to access. These brief messages, which appeared to describe what she was doing, came simultaneously to one of her other deeply connected friends and me. The friend called me up and accused me of messing with her by texting *weird* messages. I had to insist that I was also receiving these same messages at the same time. I had not originated them. One sentence I remember said, "I was exhausted and am resting well." This text came through after about two weeks. A month or so later, a subsequent message said, "I'm reviewing my life events." Then there was a big earthquake in Haiti, and we both got a text saying, "I'm helping the doctors in Haiti to save as many lives as possible." (Ellen had been a very publicly aware medical doctor.) Three or four other similar messages accounted for what Ellen might be doing in her new awareness.

Finally, one day, I remember being in the house, thinking about these unexpected experiences, and silently wondering if it would be possible to connect with her and communicate if I consulted a medium. I was shocked to receive immediately a big *YES!!!!* in my awareness at the end of that thought. All right. I decided to try it.

A friend had recommended that I do this and had given me contact information for a practicing medium, saying this woman was connected and accurate. When I had a first appointment with the medium, she appeared to communicate with Ellen and receive Ellen's messages. For instance, Ellen had promised to help me find my next life companion, and she repeated that promise through the medium. She also suggested that I sell the house I was rattling around in and buy another, smaller one. She said, "the *cute blue house with all the flowers* that is waiting for you." I didn't know what she was referring to. Using the medium brought to an end the strange text messages on Ellen's computer, and the other friend who had been receiving the same texts as I thanked me with much relief for succeeding in making them go away.

Ellen had often told me that if something happened to her, she wanted me to find another love and remarry, and she had even said that she would concentrate on finding me the right person once she was no longer in this life. I had taken this statement *with a grain of salt*, as you might imagine. But once we were halfway through the new year, 2009, I began to think that I did not want to remain single for the rest of my life. I found a person on a dating app who appeared perfect. She lived near me in Durham, NC, but had lived for over 25 years in Manhattan before moving here 20 years before.

As I explored online dating sites, I realized that I needed someone who thoroughly enjoyed the cultural and intellectual stimulation of big city and international life. I deeply loved Nature and still do. My consciousness had evolved in Ellen's and my life together, and New York had been an influential part of that evolution. I wrote to the new person but received no response. I later discovered that before I found and wrote to her, she had already quit that dating app. I was deeply disappointed.

Then, I heard from the woman who had quit the dating site! Nancy was writing spontaneously, of her own accord, from a different dating site where I had also registered. It was hard to believe! There she was! I answered quickly, putting my contact information into the message, so she could not disappear again. She replied quickly, and we made an appointment to have dinner together at a nearby restaurant the following week.

The day came, and Nancy and I both arrived in the parking lot at about the same time, driving identical gold Priuses. Weird! We introduced ourselves and sat down inside for dinner. We enjoyed good food and conversation, discovering in the process that we knew a lot of the same people in Manhattan, although we had never met each other, nor had Nancy and Ellen ever met. They just appeared to have frequented the same places simultaneously with the same friends. When it came time to exchange contact info, we pulled out identical Blackberries to record the information. I visited Nancy a couple of weeks later, then she came by my house, we marveled to discover that we shared several identical pieces of furniture, and even art pieces by the same New York artist, who had been a close friend of both Ellen and Nancy.

I was still not recovered from losing Ellen, and Nancy was still grieving the recent loss of her partner, so we were not ready to begin a committed relationship. We met about once a week for dinner, conversation, closeness for nearly a year before we felt it was time to connect our lives. In the interim, however, Nancy called me one morning, knowing that the house Ellen and I had shared was much too big for me to keep on my own. She told me that the house across the street from hers was coming onto the market. I needed to sell and move and discovered it was a *cute blue house*. It was February, so I couldn't tell about the flowers. I bought that house and moved there March 1. Starting then and continuing through the Autumn, I was delighted to discover *all the flowers* – someone previously lived there who had loved to garden and had planted many bushes that flowered in turn all year long. I enjoyed camellias in January, evolving through spirea and lilacs in spring, and altheas and crape myrtles all summer and into the fall.

Ellen and Nancy had never met in New York, that they knew, but I had to believe that Ellen had somehow helped to get the two of us acquainted with each other.

We traveled to Connecticut to marry in March of 2011 when same-sex marriage was first legal there. Then in May, we held a sizeable interfaith wedding at Nancy's church in Durham, with the loving participation of members of my church in Chapel Hill – two different Christian denominations. Both of our families also came to celebrate with us. This observance wasn't yet legal as a marriage in North Carolina. We had already legally married in Connecticut, so we just enjoyed sharing our happiness with friends and family, knowing that we were already legally joined. We have now been very happily married for more than ten years.

When Nancy and I married, we knew already that older people, when they enter a committed relationship, are no longer simply two individuals with families of origin. Instead, their new relationship includes all the individuals with whom both people have spent time in committed relationships and the families of those people. When two older people marry, it's like a coming together of two communities -- twenty or thirty people or more – often many more, when different generations, dead and alive, are added up across two extended families. Each of us brings to the new marriage the genetics and the influence of all those connected to our earlier couples: grandparents, parents, siblings, children, grandchildren, aunts, uncles, cousins, and other tribal members for both individuals.

Both Nancy and I have welcomed Ellen, and my ex-husband, Ron, and Nancy's earlier relationships into our relationship and lives. We are continuing to explore our learning, professional and personal spiritual service opportunities, and the personal enjoyments we brought to our marriage. Our lives together are rich and rewarding (and occasionally challenging, too, of course). We have been able to visit and revisit Paris once or twice a year during our marriage, enjoying bilingual and bicultural lives, activities, and friendships, as Ellen and I would have liked but didn't get to do. Together, we have continued the kind of servant leadership that marked Ellen's and my lives together, only now it is focused more on spiritual and less on physical health.

Through continuing occasional sessions with the medium, I have learned that as my consciousness has been evolving here on earth, Ellen has been growing in her awareness in the dimension where she finds herself. She is much less attentive to daily details here than she was initially. She remains available to connect with Nancy and my needs, delights, and questions whenever we create that opportunity for communication with a session. Over that same ten-plus years, I have become much more connected in my awareness, knowing ahead of time whatever I'll learn in a session with the medium. No longer is Ellen the primary source of information about what we're experiencing. She now is present while all of us hear and learn from some venerable, wise angel or master or group of souls from the higher dimension.

Another wonderful outcome of my deep grief for Ellen happened when I finally said *yes* to my lifelong calling to become qualified as a spiritual leader. All my life, each time I'd experienced a life change, I had felt called to attend a seminary and become ordained. In the weeks and months following Ellen's passing, this question had come up again, inevitably. This time, it happened after I had been emulating Ellen by meditating daily, knowing that this practice had brought her deep peace. In the physical dimension, my life up till then had disappeared with Ellen. I no longer had a reason to say *no* and thus no longer resisted. In addition, Nancy was showing me the way, as she had already answered a call to become a chaplain and had enrolled in her denomination's local minister training program, with a couple of semesters at a respected seminary in Pennsylvania. I found myself really envying her. When I visited her once for the weekend, I was meditating in the seminary chapel and the voice inside me said, forcefully, "It's time for YOU to go to seminary too,!!" I meekly said "Yes", and enrolled at One Spirit Interfaith Seminary in New York City.

This was the beginning of a wonderful new period. Although already over 70, I felt completely at home and my life finally began to integrate again. Both Nancy and I started our marriage with complementary new missions for pastoral care and leadership.

I have appreciated this ongoing opportunity to deepen my awareness of our power as humans in this dimension. The better we humans, collectively, can tune into creation and the needs of fellow human and non-human creatures along with ourselves, the more successfully we will experience happiness and joy each day in the higher spiritual dimension.

I feel deeply blessed to have had this learning opportunity with Ellen and then with Nancy and Ellen. How much my awareness has changed just in the 13 years since Ellen and I parted ways in November, 2008! I look forward to each present moment, in which I can keep increasing my resonance with all that is, as I learn to tune in increasingly well to higher and higher frequencies of awareness!

The following poem expresses well my life in this moment:

Waking Thought, July 6 2021

A beautiful day – still pure potential – waiting to be opened—

That was my waking thought.

I opened my eyes,

Coming to first awareness,

Seeing sunlight --

The purity of a day not yet experienced,

When I might choose whatever thoughts I wish,

Create moments of delight,

Enjoy connecting with my friends and family,

Breathe deep into my loving heart and blissful soul,

Think whatever will align me with the life I wish..

Now I know the magic of expressed desire,

And the power of imagining in Peace –

I use the Universal Laws.

I pause, I smile, I enjoy, I thank – relaxing to allow this day's

Unfolding.

I am happy being here right now!

ROSEMARY C. HYDE

ABOUT THE AUTHOR

Rosemary Hyde and Ellen Scheiner met late in life – Rosemary was 59 and Ellen 66. Both had experienced previous long-term relationships starting in youth. And both had eventually realized that they had grown far apart from their then partners, in terms of beliefs, values, and goals.

Rosemary was discovering, after moving away from her heterosexual marriage, that gay relationships were possible. Upon seeing many lesbian couples after she had arrived in Oakland, CA, she experienced a flash of insight that helped her understand why she had never fit comfortably into the heterosexual world. Ellen, having grown up in cosmopolitan New York City, had realized her gender orientation in early adulthood. Ellen was able to instruct Rosemary on the details of Lesbian culture. This was very useful to Rosemary.

Both Ellen and Rosemary had completed academic

careers, Rosemary in culture and communications, and Ellen in medicine. Both were avid Francophiles who spoke easy French, as they had both lived and studied in French- speaking European countries. Both were deeply attuned to healing, Ellen as a physician and Rosemary as an alternative healer -- a classical homeopath. Both were poets. Both had devoted themselves to nurturing spiritual and emotional growth in younger people and wished to continue doing so. Both had been academics, devoted to learning and finding deep fulfillment in teaching.

Both Rosemary and Ellen, sharing an adventurous willingness to try something new, had decided to commit to each other. Immediately after that decision, Ellen received a diagnosis of recurrent Stage 4 (metastatic) breast cancer, with a prognosis of six months to live. Together they decided they would still go ahead with the ceremony, and were fortunate to experience a total of almost ten years together as committed soulmates and practice partners.

Ellen died, unexpectedly, of cardiac arrest, on election night, 2008. Rosemary's solace, in response to the trauma of loss, was to surrender to her grief, a decision that led into a world of heightened sensitivity and poetry. She recorded poems as they came to her – a window into the primal experience of shock and grief and the human ability to transcend old beliefs and to accept new awareness at a higher spiritual level.

As a homeopath, Rosemary knew the healing value of situations to heal those experiencing a similar situation – grief soothing grief. Thus, she determined to share the poems with others by finding a publisher, so the poems could become a healing resource for people in the grip of sorrow – a situation that most humans experience at least a few times. She envisions that reading these poems may offer healing to each reader who is mourning an important loss.

All losses bring grief. Whether we are losing a cherished dream, admitting that we can no longer practice a beloved occupation or pastime, parting ways with a life partner, experiencing the death of a dear companion or spouse, or starting to process our own inevitable departure from earthly attachments, we grieve. It's no use running away from our feelings. They are a gift and a doorway to new and deeper love and insight. In embracing each opportunity for transformation, we find over and over that what we thought was lost has only changed its appearance. Love never disappears: it just deepens. In these poems, Rosemary shares with readers her own path to discovering love continuing on the other side of loss. She invites you, too, to revise your own sad experiences of loss as you revisit the tumult of rebalancing that you, too, have navigated repeatedly. When you surrender to the feelings and the experience, they will lead you to transformation, to integration, to greater strength and deeper peace.

May you be happy, healthy, and fulfilled as you walk this path of Love.

DISCUSSION GUIDE
FOR BOOK CLUBS, SUPPORT GROUPS AND SELF-REFLECTION

A traumatic experience can seem overwhelmingly tragic. However, the human spirit responds to an energy larger and more powerful than itself, and hope points us toward the possibility of renewing life.

This guide highlights ways you might use these poems as a basis for finding greater joy after grieving over losses of people, relationships, major possessions, roles, possibilities, and other precious gifts of life. Our experiences derive directly from how we choose to perceive life events. We can always see the "glass" half full or half empty. That's the nature of material life. In the Universal perspective, everything helps us toward greater joy – when we let that happen.

Please use this guide to help you discover the rich personal resources that new awareness can put within your reach.

1. Dr. Elizabeth Kubler-Ross was the first person, in 1969, in her classic book, *On Death and Dying,* to describe and analyze how people experience grief. She developed a model called "Five Stages of Grief." The five stages are: denial, anger, bargaining, depression and acceptance. We do not experience all these emotions in any fixed sequence or time frame. As you read the different poems, which ones fit into these categories? How do stages occur or recur? Is there a fixed sequence?
2. How did these poems fit within your own experiences of grief?
3. Are there poems that do not fit into any of Kubler-Ross's stages of grief? Which poems? What category would you create for each of these "outlier" poems?
4. When the poet attended a "grief support group," she learned that to resolve acute grief, she needed to "integrate" the loss into a newly defined and organized life after loss. Different poems describe aspects of "integrating" or adjusting – finding new ways of thinking and being, where old thoughts and feelings are transforming. In the poems, in what areas of life were old beliefs and feelings transforming into a new way of being?
5. In poems that have a touch of humor, how do you feel the humorous interpretation of events is helpful or unhelpful on the path toward integration? What other tools besides

humor seem to be helpful in moving toward a time of more hopeful, positive feelings?

6. What consistencies, inconsistencies, and conflicts do you notice in the writer's experience of grief?

7. In several poems, the poet uses images to describe what Ellen meant to her. List the images you find. Is there a theme? Think about someone you've loved and lost, and create a short list of images that describe who that person was for you.

8. We grieve many losses in our lives, not just people leaving. What other losses have caused you to experience grieving as you reintegrated into your next life phase? Were these losses random or did they relate to your stage of life?

9. In the poems, the writer ended up beginning to see how she would be stronger and better able to move forward after the period of grieving ends. Describe how she sees that happening.

10. Looking back on losses you've grieved in your own life, what tools have you used to retrieve new strength and energy from the remains of the old life you had and lost?

11. These poems chronicle a brief, intense time during which the poet purposefully allowed herself to experience freely whatever feelings occurred, in the order in which they occurred. She chose this path of non-resistance knowing that resistance of any kind slows down needed progress forward toward resolution of issues. In what ways, during

the six weeks when the poems were written, do you see progress occurring toward Kubler-Ross's final stage of "acceptance?"

12. When you first saw the title and cover of this book, what were your expectations? How were these expectations fulfilled or changed because of reading the poems? How were your ideas about grieving confirmed or changed?

13. Sometimes people stipulate that they don't want any ceremonial event marking their passing. Given the role that Ellen's "Perfect New York Cocktail Party" played for her wife and friends as they processed losing her, can you think of reasons why a person might or might not choose to give some directions for celebrating life? Problems tend to occur through two-sided conflicts or contradictions. For the poet, the conflict was her previous enjoyment of life with Ellen, and her new focus on how sad it was to live without Ellen. Solutions often come about by applying a third force that creates something new and positive from the previously opposing experiences. Often a ritual involving sharing with others can provide the solution. Rituals can create new, positive energy from the disconnected fragments surrounding a loss. For the poet and for Ellen's other close friends, the cocktail party celebrating Ellen's life helped to create helpful new communication and friendship. How might you (even retroactively) find it helpful to create and

carry out a ritual marking a painful ending you've experienced so that a new beginning becomes easier?

14. How do the spiritual values expressed in the poems agree or disagree with your personal values? Did the poems help you develop any new understanding?

15. The poet talked in the Foreword about the homeopathic principle that "Like cures Like" and how knowing that principle led her to seek out other people's writings that might echo the grief she was feeling. Did you find reading these poems helpful in processing any grieving you might be experiencing, even if the event happened a long time ago? How might you use this principle of "Like cures Like" to help you integrate and release any other feelings you'd like to move beyond? This homeopathic process works for sadness, anger, anxiety, fear – any feeling, really.

16. During the weeks that the poet was chronicling her process of integration, she felt compelled to share her experiences, sometimes in three or four poems a day that were very different one from the other. Feelings are like clouds crossing the sky. They can arrive and leave very quickly. Writing the poems was helpful to her as a way of sharing these fleeting experiences with an imagined audience even when a real-time human audience was not available. For her, poetry was the most natural expressive activity. The arts are an important facilitator for releasing feelings, and so are other creative activities. What would be your

preferred kind of creative expression for releasing negative feelings? When and how will you test this idea for yourself?

17. Thinking about what you imagined about Ellen from the poems, how well do you think you might recognize her (if she were still living) if you happened to meet her at an event? Think about a person you are close to, and list things that are important to you about that person. How well does that describe the person that others in more casual situations would recognize? What do you think your closest, most beloved person (or pet) knows about you that others might not know? How does your beloved other see you differently than you see yourself? Do you think it is possible to know someone from a perspective other than our individual experience?

18. Three meaningful dreams are described in the poems. How do you think the dreamer's feelings and thoughts translated into the images described from the dreams? What did you learn about the dreamer from the dream descriptions? Try to remember a meaningful dream that you have experienced, and think about how it affected you as you thought about it or shared it with someone else.

19. Several poems allude to the huge contrast between what Ellen thought of herself and, as they were celebrating her life, what other people thought of her. Think of some negative trait you think you have and then reflect on

whether your evaluation of yourself is supported by any evidence from how other people act or what they have told you. How well do you understand how others see you?

20. When someone dies, we tend to believe they are just gone from our everyday experience. The poet came to believe during these weeks of grieving that instead, after dying physically, an individual has traveled to a different dimension. Communication between the person still on earth and the person who has transitioned seemed to continue, in different ways than before. Both parties need to engage in a learning curve to experience a sense of reconnection. If you have ever lost someone close to you, in what ways have you experienced them since their physical death? Have such perceptions in any way led you to modify your previous beliefs about living and dying?

21. In reflecting on your beliefs and thoughts about life, about yourself, about your feelings, about death and dying, about integrating a loss and moving forward (or about any other important topic that seems relevant), have your views and experience changed since reading these poems? How?

22. What lines from the poems stood out to you as ones you would like to remember and apply in your own life?

In the years since these poems were written and their publication, the writer has shared them with many people who were experiencing grief after having lost someone they deeply loved. In every case, the individuals in grief have found reading the poems helpful in reducing their sad, angry, or fearful feelings as they negotiated the twists and turns of grieving. If you know someone who has recently lost a beloved person, you might want to offer that person a copy of these poems to help them, as well.

Thank you!!

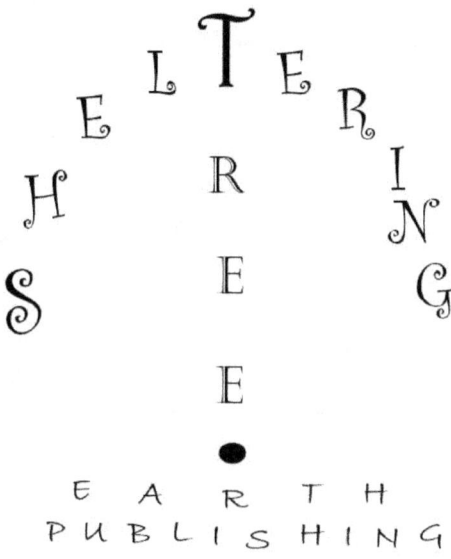

We are an exclusive publishing house.

Our readers, once they finish one of our books, will be able to get up and face the world wiser, stronger, centered, and know that we are not alone: we are all a part of the Sheltering Tree on Earth.

If you feel that calling, please refer to

ShelteringTree.Earth/writer-guidelines

www.ingramcontent.com/pod-product-compliance
Lightning Source LLC
LaVergne TN
LVHW020934090426
835512LV00020B/3358